MEDITERRANEAN

MEDITERRANEAN

Jenni Daiches

SCOTTISH CONTEMPORARY POETS SERIES

SCOTTISH CULTURAL PRESS

First published 1995
by Scottish Cultural Press
PO Box 106, Aberdeen AB9 8ZE
Tel: 01224 583777
Fax: 01224 575337

British Library Cataloguing in Publication Data
A catalogue record for this book is available from the British Library

ISBN: 1 898218 35 8

The publisher acknowledges subsidy from the Scottish Arts Council
towards the publication of this volume

Printed and bound by
BPC-AUP Aberdeen Ltd, Aberdeen

Contents

Born in 1941 in Chicago, of Scottish parents, Jenni Daiches was educated in America and England. After obtaining degrees in English from the Universities of Cambridge and London, she began a career in teaching and freelance writing.

From 1968 to 1971, Jenni lived in Kenya, where she taught for a year at the University of Nairobi. Since 1971 she has lived in Scotland, though she has travelled and lectured in the USA, Africa, China and Europe. She has two daughters and a son.

From 1963 to 1982 Jenni was married to Angus Calder, and as Jenni Calder she has written over a dozen books on aspects of English, Scottish and American literature and history. Although she published a few poems as a student, it is only in the last 10 years that Jenni has been writing poetry seriously, and *Mediterranean* is her first full-length collection. She says that her poetry arises mainly out of everyday experiences of life and work, and is much influenced by place and landscape.

She is now Head of Publications at the National Museum of Scotland and is currently working on a biography of Naomi Mitchison.

for Rachel, Gowan and Gideon

Acknowledgements

The author and publisher wish to thank the editors of the following publications in which some of these poems have already appeared:

Chapman, Lines Review, Northwords, PN Review, Scotia Bar Anthology 1991, Setting Forth, Spectrum.

With thanks to the School of Poets, who nourished this collection.

READING BY A WINDOW

My finger catches the edge of a page,
and through the glass half-grown boys
play shinty, calling like crows, spinning
the ball across the grass. The paper
flutters the peaceful print. I am greedy
for words, cram and taste them, loose
them, reckless, into the bloodstream. A boy
pivots on his heel, an arm wide
as a wing. The water behind his head
blends cloud and supple islands.

Gulls balance above the boys'
swooping awkwardness. History
wheels. With my book open in my hands
the glass reveals a rehearsal of the past,
of boys shouting and turning, a boat
braced on the loch. For boys have run
on this shore since stories began, and wind
has driven the sails of the herring hunters.

The page settles, now cradling the tranquil
print. But the words are restive, shake
the window, call like boys or crows.
Spindles of smoke roll on the shore,
blurring the fire and the salt-bleached wood.
Under a diffident sun the boys
throw their bodies on the ground. The page
traps their breaking voices, suddenly
holds them hostage for the coming story.

IN A CONFUCIAN TEMPLE WITH LAO TSU

Here is a place an old man can read the paper
in peace. I am ashamed at my haste.
It is all too soon, too fast. A basket of garlic
passes. Bicycle wheels turn gracefully.
Ants are eloquent under the twisted tree.

Time? Measured by water clocks and temple
pillars? Marking the rhythm of feet that take
me between rooted sentinels? Chained to the sun,
imprisoned in the moon? Time here is liquid
dried to dust, powdered on the paving stones.

Each grain a thousand years, each year stirred
by my steps, clouding my skin, a cloak on my tongue.
The hours run in silence. Wheels tick-tick
across the courtyard. The girl's black eyes don't blink –
my stare irrelevant, my presence nothing.

I contemplate. The old man turns a page.
His spectacles have slipped. Each revolution
of the wheel scores another track on his lean
landscape. The tread imprints the palms of my hands.
Time prevents me reaching out to touch.

The mind also turns. Thoughts like blown petals
skittishly revolve and overthrow.
I consider if I want his gentle virtue.
Order and understanding, Lao Tsu – where
are they? Did you cheat authority?

Here I could stay. Shut my eyes beneath
the scholar's tree and live within until
time dissolved each blue vein and finger
nail, each fold of brain, each knuckle, each
bone masked in muscle, toe and heel,
the furrowed lip and every unborn word.
Tick-tick. Slowly the wheel turns. Almost
I become an atom of a grain – but can't escape.
Spinning in this plenitude of years I am
too quick, too indistinct, too soon, too late.

RAIN AT BRACKLEY

They weren't the stones we were seeking
but they leapt out of the fine rain
and etched their silence on us, not able
to shoulder so heavy a weight of water.

Each stone was headed with a bold fishing
boat, eagle-keen on the bright
granite, taut as if flying not floating
in the green glen. Such young men.

On the quay at Carradale the orange
nets are heaped into small hills
and looped tractor tyres make rock-
hoppers to skim the rough sea bed

and scoop up scallops. The boats are tied
in twos and threes, crusted with salt
and fish scales, coils of rope, flakes
of oozing rust beading the paint.

Such young men, dying in their own nets,
hauled to deep silence. In the rain
at Brackley we noticed they live long,
but not the *Antares* men who drowned.

THE GATHERERS

The creak of oilskins echoes the seabird's cry.
The shore is a tangled garden of mussels. They grow

as if to reach where the light begins. Until
in the evening the gatherers come. Beyond the rim

of sand and rock the grass falters. The hollow
of a noust is empty of boats, the scattered stones

of what were once walls are printed with fire.
An otter has left a salmon's skull and a trail

of broken sea urchins, pretty fragments fringed
in salty sea pink. We are gatherers. April's

lengthening sun is cut by the scrape of a knife.
A flint or the sharp edge of a shell would do

as well, as they did, millennia ago. Eider,
white and black, stipple the seamless water.

With what elemental wisdom they build their nests
and feed their frantic young. With what skill

does the otter make its kill. With what comfort
do the gatherers harvest from the abundant rock.

SHADOW ON THE WATER

Swaledale, April 1992

The trees are woven into the river
bank, nameless without leaves, lean
and black, alive beneath their bark.

We walk by the water. The sun drops
towards the fell and casts our shadows
back, to lie on tangled grass.

We walk on a narrow path. The sun
splinters the running river. We stop,
greedy for light, mouths and hands

unmasked, unfolded. The running river
spins a web beyond brilliance,
but we see no more than sun and water

and the shape of trees, a trick of the dark,
an illusion of print stilled on the current,
as if held in the air, untouched by water.

REFLECTION

Feathers of candle
flame divide the grains
of darkness.
In the glass
two faces
obliquely lit like moons.

They seem to be flesh.
The faithful glass
refuses to define.
Fire laps images
alive as water.
They are figured in the eyes
of one another.

The parent and the child
in every lover.
They seem to drown
in oceanic glass,
the light returns
a garment, adrift,
swinging with the tide.

SPIDER

That night the spider veiled a corner
of the kitchen with a web that caught
and held the morning
light. Its shimmer
was the moon on water, sun on downy
skin. I unravelled half-remembered
dreams. The threads in wonderful
suspense, spanning wall to wall. I sat
drinking tea, and saw your blunder,
your blind entry, your brushing away
of the cloudy world of sleep, and the drift
of filament thicken the sunlit air.
I held my cup and remembered the half-
remembered, the mesh of dream and morning,
the imploding weave of my life and yours.

DEFINITION

Definition, but no colour, no black,
no white. Precise, clear as water,
but inconceivable as flesh,
out of touch, unreal.
The wheelchair hushed as feathers,
the memory, spectral,
but stronger than the body, lifted,
tended, warm but hands
adrift, weak as petals.
Her voice a degree beyond silence.
'I'd forgotten it was so beautiful.'
And it was beautiful,
the August afternoon, the sun-
burnished barley, the last light of her eye.

SHORE

interpret the water
slow as melting glass
below the improbable
flight of a red-legged
comedian

summer rain
hangs in fine arrest

this early the world
is private the splash
of a tossed oyster shell
eclipses sound

there are no prints
before mine far out
a single yacht
is in suspense
the subtle tide retreats

the tree at the headland
stares back from silence
there is no face
in the water or words
raked in the sand

BESIDE THE LIFFEY

Beside the Liffey
she moves her meagre legs.
Her skirt is lavender,
her jacket crushed a little
but each button tight.
Her umbrella's broken ribs
inhibit her uprightness.
Its wings sag against
the rain which damages
the velvet of her hat.

Her ragged fingers and her face
are white as skin on milk.
She takes three steps.
Her eyes are straight and wide.
The Liffey thickly floats
half of Dublin to the sea.

And now three paces back.
The umbrella trembles,
O'Connell Bridge remains.
Forward she goes, and backward,
over and over, seriously.

The debris-weighted river
passes on. The city's
shabby stone is debonair.
Gulls fold and bend above her.
Three careful steps
to give the lie to time.
The day is on the ebb.
Forward the measured march
towards the dark, and back.

VILLAGE

The shale waste lies like a half-eaten
beast while the morning coaxes each
doorway and shop window from retreat.
Dawn unwraps a single street
that blindly obeys the contour of the ridge.
Blurred profiles of stone acquire an edge,

and become the cavernous Co-op with ramparts
of catfood and cornflakes, the used
car dealer and the post office dog-eared
with galactic magazines, the bus
shelter, the baker's thick
with yeast, the doctor's papered with warnings
of pregnancy and death
from cigarettes and neat
notices of cancer smears, the chemist
where cures can be collected and dust
clings to talc and bubblebath. It's years
since the mines tumbled out their oily earth.

All on a spine that at night is lit
like an arch of stars but now slowly leans
towards midday with prams and old men
who once worked and young who haven't
waiting to be taken somewhere else.
The hours fall from noon until
the children on their fitful way from school
sling bricks and beercans into the canal.

HORSE IN GLASGOW

A horse comes out of the dark,
graith a-glitter in the light
and rain, haunches heavy
and steady, hoofs striking
the street like full buckets.

Beside the huge dipping
head walks a man, fingers
linked in wet leather,
silent as an old friend.

And we two turn to watch
their remote and measured way,
in Glasgow, and almost touch.
The space between holds wordless
praise for the great beast
for a moment possessing the city.

People churn and spill
against the perfect pulse
ringing into the dark.

WASHINGTON: DEER CROSSING

salve dear xing
dazzled by avenues I whistle
an old blues and think
dear xing of you

it's a white city but the river
and the boys who wheel
around my feet are brown
and so is the driver
of the Washington Flyer and when
the brakes give out he's calm and
says he'll do the best he can

and so is the man who wants
to take my picture but I
am faithful dear xing

in Virginia's mud
stands Ulysses S Grant
with guts on his boots
he was a poor politician

oh freedom
no wonder they go mad and kill
here megalomania is beautiful

we fly
down the Mall in syn-
chronicity with museums
no wonder I
and presidents have illusions

the frontier is reformed
the wilderness is dead

the brown man with a camera
asks me to go to bed
xing boom
xing you are my sunshine
alone in America
I think of you dear xing

JEWISH CEMETERY, FRANKFURT

Deep autumnal green has soaked the earth.
Through the barred gate it invites like velvet,
beckons an intrusion under the awkward
arms of the broad old trees, boldly red,
frailly yellow as a night's alluring moon.
The wall is also old, its rough centuries warm
to the hand. The people passing would think it odd
if a woman rested her head against it and wept.
The trees are helpless within the spiralled leaves.
Beyond are the stones, huddled, dark, leaning
to the right, the left, forward, shawled in the light
of a lenient afternoon. Their faces void,
their grey garments folded close. I listen.
I believe there's a thread of ancient song. The city
takes a breath. The trams, the river traffic, the market
stalls, dissolve. I smell the fire and the blood,
the acrid smoke of fear. Where once a temple
stood some simple words confine catastrophe.
If only I had love enough for all.

MEDITERRANEAN

This island is almost Asia.
The blue is Iznik, or in the pause
of breath between day and deep night Persia.
The green, frayed by the heat, is a plain
beaten to dust by beasts and herdsmen.
The light is silk, the walls carnelian.

The cliff-edge monastery is almost
Islam, in the place of the apostle who was almost
a Jew. These fishermen unwitting
Europeans, Europe an invention.

The courtyard spills with blossom,
a kitchen chair stands
empty in the sun. Cats
on the steps, one, two, three,
as if they know who I am. The door
half-open to a shaft of darkness. I discover
I am somewhere in the centre.

Mediterranean. Behind,
the ancestors moving through cloud,
bravely creating God. Around,
the riders of the sea. The tideless
water dissolves the pathways of crusades
by traders, thieves and soldiers.
Before, the years waiting for release,
a life unmapped, unfigured.

Summer is leaving. By the harbour
the bars are shuttered, the beach
almost empty. The red is wine,
the grey the workshop's smoke, silver
longing's brittle armour.
Mediterranean. Held
somewhere in the centre,
like warmth in raw stone.
Watching the year ebb
until time and purpose join.

GALE FORCE

The ship pitches cups and spoons across
the galley and pulls drawers from their sockets.
The wind wakens me.
My house is also a ship.

I am quite safe, he says
from the call box by the harbour.
His voice inhabits my head, safe as houses.

I am awake as the wind
grapples my walls
and shouts at my door.
I am alright, he says from the box by the harbour.

The seas rear
over my roof. I wait
for the crash. I'll fix
whatever needs fixing, he writes from the engine room.
I look for salt spray on the paper.
All I can see are fifty-foot waves
throwing a tangle of radar into the gale.

Hail beats at the glass.
The water is dark.
The ship shies at the lurching squall.
He writes letters as the engines and the waves
pound. Safe as houses, safe
as a port in a storm, safe
as words finding a harbour in my head.

SCOTLAND UPSIDEDOWN

A whale's back breaks
the grey shimmer of the ocean
in summer. A black sheen
as if dug from deep in the water.
An arch like a boulder,
or an architect's dream.

I can see from north to south –
believe me – here on the bridge
by the captain's side. I can smell
mountains streaked with quartz
and snow, and bladed rivers.

The whale crosses
our southward path. The gulls
wheel away to the skerries.
The wind is westerly,
like the whale who blows and dives.

From here I see a squall
skid on the firth and darken
the green strath. Empty rooms
have turned their faces to the wall,
and the walls have fallen.

Whole cities have their roots
in the air, the dust on my tongue.
The way to look at this country,
from the dipping prow of a ship,
north at her back.

I've turned the map around.
Now south is up, and the far shore
is where we begin.

COCKLEROY

So small a hill to reveal
a nation. I know where the sea
admits the ships of centuries.
I know salt and coal, clay,
the ocean's oil, the rust
red shale. Although mist
masks the firth I feel
the muscle of history.

A serpent of fire is frozen
above Grangemouth. Plumes
of smoke are caught in painterly
stillness. A palace
has shrugged off its roof.

Snow has drizzled the smooth
shoulders of the Ochils. Beyond,
mountains I can name,
Vorlich, Ledi, Lomond,
white-headed, hard masters.

Fingers of cloud rest
below hill forts and burial
places. Spectres of old
forests gather at the rivers
that turned wheels and sped shuttles.

The march to a hundred battles
passed below. Preachers travelled
in words, cadgers' ponies
carried cloth and chapbooks.
Sweated messengers bore news
of the deaths of queens and kings.

From Cockleroy the land offers
trails of black cattle where the hind
once fled. Canals, causeways
of grain and cannon. Railways
raised by the grace of viaducts.
Highways where barley was sickle-cut.

I tread earth barely allayed
by the winter light. On this hill
I name the particulars of a nation.

LEAVING SCOTLAND

The plough and the harvester have etched
the land. Its quilted particularity
needle-sharp, its colours filling
the heart. Umber, tender brown,
moleskin, fox red, bracken and barley.
The earth falls. I am on my way.

> The *Hector* drawn
> by the sun out of the mouth
> of Loch Broom, servant
> to the winds. Her ribs
> enter the bodies
> of the two hundred. The ocean
> shivers their thin dreams,
> the spray's hiss tears
> the words on their tongues.
> They have hardly begun.

We tilt into cloud that blurs one part
of my world. Leaving that land's lack
of grace, its spitting discord, water
on hot coals. The sky opens.
A thousand wonders disclosed, loch
and mountain, radical alchemy of rock
and light, fusion of limit and distance.

> It has ended.
> Each generation grafted
> to soil, to sea loch, to river.
> The wake of the *Hector*
> furrows their love, the sails
> heavy as grief. Eyes
> follow a path from the east.

Leaving the cryptic city, the boy
begging at the steps, effulgent minds
dulled by crack and drink, women
dancing together to the music of men.

Blown far to the north,
beaten to Newfoundland,
then hirpling south
to the crooked finger
that was named Nova Scotia.
They have cattle and ploughs.
They have oatmeal for the first winter
which waits, a wolf
beyond the ring of fire.
They have axes and scar
their hands with the felling of trees.
The *Hector* escapes the roar
of Arctic ice.

Niagara below me, a glittering palace
of spindrift. We prepare the return to earth
and curve over the shore of the great
lake. I walk in another city
and find Scotland in the necropolis,
the proof roughly cut in stone.
The evening splinters a rowan
into a myriad monarch butterflies.
Below this prism of lustrous red
on red I read the abradant past.

They hack into the dark
forest under the dying
leaves. As they draw sap
from the maple and fish
from the water Gaelic unwinds
from their lips. Song
spills and runs.
A young man wraps his plaid
on his arm and kills
a deer in the snow.
The blood warms him.

Geese skein on the burning tail
of August. The road is a hundred miles
of wheat stubble, the huge barns
shelter a year's labour. On and on.
Leaving the learning of stone on a dyke,
and the plough that heals the battlefield.
The *Hector*'s two hundred never return.
They send home for granite to build.

JEWISH CEMETERY, PRAGUE

The rooks repair their nests,
wings black ensigns at the bare trees.
You build high in a city.

These graves are built high.
In the small space awarded more earth
was heaped for layered burials.
The crowded stones reach up like hands,

towards the black convocation, the blue
beyond the synagogues. The dead
have held their own for half a millennium.

The memorials tilt with age.
Held their own at the crossroads,
remained when the living were taken away,
remained each time the tanks came.

Perhaps it was a poet who chiselled
language so deep, as if each letter
had been lifted to harbour in the heart.

The trees are tall. The birds
are calling and building. My thoughts
turn on those who have no resting
place, no earth, no stone, no words.

REMEMBER MOSTAR

Remember Mostar?
That pretty hillside town.
Here are the holiday snaps –
look, the children on the bridge,
the domes diamonds of sun.

The basket bought at the roadside
is in my kitchen now,
filled with potatoes and onions.
Remember the mosque, and walking
barefoot on the cool stone?

Remember Mostar.
Prayer is roofless now, the trees
stand in rags, the girl's skin
is fretted with shrapnel wounds.
Look, where the bandages bleed.

MUSEUM PEACE

In the half dark
collector's appetite and designer's art-
ifice evaporate. Peace has come
to the house of acquisition.

This is my reward
when labour stretches into night.
A glimmer of bone, a glint of brass
in neglected crannies of light.

An arc of ivory,
an engine in unnatural rest, briefly
beyond the possessive custodian,
and the visitor not allowed to understand.

The hand held out
to me is stone, the smile is cast
in bronze, but now it is almost
as if the pulse runs.

As if snow leopard's
tongue lolls and crocodile closes
his jaws. The silence is not death,
but a palpable holding of breath.

Perhaps they are dancing.
So what if the music is a clash
of continents, and glass cases crash
and limbs are without grace.

But it's only my footfall
tolling the day's end. Siva
and the Buddha consort with Allah,
and the door secures a place of peace.

FALLS

The thrum of water climbs the sloping grass.
Below, a vibrant hiss and rumble more lively
than the sun. The louping river bravely
spills from a silky lip of rock, drops
white skeins of water keen as blades
or slivered glass, beaded with splintered light.

Someone, doubtless, can tell how many millions
of centuries carved this chasm, and doubtless science
explains our eyes trapped in the black boiling
which rises to meet the woven water, seeming
still but moving, arrested but free, clean-
edged as sculpture, but impossible to capture.

We have not come as far as the years suggest.
The sun skims the crystals from the snow.
Warmth milks the earth, sets the water
to run. The lean trees whose roots claw
the scarted cliff are not as dead as they look.
The river releases the kindness in the rock.

ON BEINN AN EOIN

This is the oldest rock, this cauldron
of scalding winds, sandstone
churned by fire and flayed by ice.
Rock subtle with lichen, the seams
of peat stitched with tormentil and orchid.

The June sun has thrown a rainbow
over the shoulder of Beinn Eighe,
and Boasbheinn is fresh with snow.
I am too young to have business
here. My peat-hag prints are shallow.

It's my fiftieth year. My climb on the mountain's
bones maps the landscape's millions.
Its wisdom draws blood from my hands.
Its great age seethes in the wind.
Below darkness rolls in the river bed.

There is no battle. I am too young
to take on a mountain, to conquer the turreted
stone. I have not felt as deep
as the light that shivers the high head
of Liatach, though I say I have suffered.

I cross a bulwark swayed and smoothed
as if time is gentle. The rough path
consents. Inside the wind the rock
is held in silence and my boots ring.
I am welcome, although I am young.

VOICES

A voice grew in the woods, searching
for moccasin prints and arrow heads.
In the soft ground, woven from wind
and tree bark, the sound of the Iroquois.

But in the creek the language of Vilna,
of Kiev, of Leeds and Liverpool, of Warsaw.

The Indian corn is dry as paper. The barley
is an ocean. The words blossomed
a welcome at Nethermills and named fish
by the dead lighthouse on Cullen pier.

But in the burn the songs of Iberia,
of Jerusalem, of noble Amsterdam.

The breathy whisper of the fen mist
and in the classroom the muddy dirge
of learning. This was the language
of never arriving, of trial.

But the slow river remembered Chicago,
New York, the woods and lakes of Cayuga.

The weaver birds at the window, the Rift
insistent on gods. The songs of Africa
leaving the white woman on the rim
of the thirsty crust of earth.

But on the hot edge of the Indian Ocean
a ballad of the plough and the herring shoals.

The performance of the past, the child,
the girl beginning, the wishes hidden
in wife and mother, and the mind spinning
a language ample and strong like silk.

While the firth murmurs in all the old voices,
gathers farmer and rabbi, red and black,
infant and mother, hunter and lover,
pupil and thinker, lullaby, lament
and praise, and carries them all to the sea.

CARRADALE

We walked to the sea. I thought,
she has walked to the sea a thousand
times. Over the fence,
among the fat lambs,

through dark rhododendrons,
down the rough path bound
with broom and perfect thistles.
My hand disregarded.

The curved shore accepted
the restless water. I thought,
she has seen the almost still
ripple a thousand times.

And Ailsa Craig, far out,
afloat, a cone of mirror
glass, misting over
as if eyes were warm breath.

The beaded rim of sea
fretted at our feet. I said,
the tide is on the ebb,
but she knew better than I

the way the earth turns.
She said, I cannot join
the fishing as I used to do.
And we walked back, along

the pitted path, over
the fence, and she broke off
the last ragged petal
of rhododendron as we went.

ARDPATRICK

By the ferryman's house at Ardpatrick
the rippled skin of water draws
cool winter yellow
from the reach of western sky.

Rough stones march
into the loch. Men hewed
and moved them, and women,
no doubt, comforted the men.

In the ferryman's garden an empty swing
rocks as if stirred by more than the wind.
A lifeboat, upturned,
a trellis of rust,
reverts tenderly to the ground,
having saved lives
and sheltered wood for the fire.

EAGLE

The path a ligament, horizontal,
cutting the cliff, and only us,
one by one, high over the dark
clutch of tide and ocean pulse.

Twelve miles of wind and water
and layers of light between the Mull
and Antrim. One step south and we'd fall
from this Highland ultimate. Two is twice

the singular, yet small in the face
of headlong rock even if embraced,
small against the unutterable colour
of sea, infinitessimal measured

by the women who walked here once and washed
in the burn, nothing in the circle of the dun,
in the shadow cast by the eagle who hangs
a sweep of wing between us and the sun.

SEPTEMBER

We take a path through a dry whisper of wheat.
It reaches above our waists and grazes our arms,
for we've folded back our sleeves to catch the September
sun. I know that skin, roughened by salt
and wind, smooth and pale where protection begins.

The air tastes of grain. You've milled an ear
of wheat in your hand and ripeness rises almost
like smoke. There's a ragged wall to climb, and a leap
to soft earth under the pines. It takes years
to learn such free and easy limber ways.

A birch lets go a yellow leaf or two.
There's a burn to wade across as if we were children.
Our own children are gone and we rediscover
the cool savour of moving water, of lying
on a green bank in the warm autumn light.

We find a way again, though I cannot read
the landscape with your eyes. There are two of us.
The season tempers stone and ripens grain.
Bodies that have mapped remote terrain
have grown enough to know that one is one.

STARLINGS

That year began with a clatter
of starlings and a walk
with our backs to the water
and its brave traverse.

A paintwater dirty day,
leaking from the sky's palette
onto naked ploughland.
The starlings, tealeaf
birds blown from the rooftops
dark as beached whales.

Godspeed old time,
old friend, blessings on
the ship of shadows that slides
beneath the conquering bridge.
Think of when the birds
poured into a cradle of cloud
and the year began.

A cold knifeblade day
shearing our dreams.
We walked with as many years
as birds blackening
the paintwater sky.

Goodbye old friend,
old time. Remember when the birds
bickered like battlefields
and the year began.

GOATHLAND

In Goathland, without a thousand browns
moor and river are unknown,
beyond people like us.
'Brown' will not do
for water taking its colours
from the earth and from light
intercepted by trees, or for the furls
of latent heather and the pliant peat
that make the moor.

So we walk along the Roman road
and don't say much, perhaps thinking
only of our boots striking
slabs of stone laid
two millennia ago. Ahead,
my daughters and my son. 'Love'
will not do for their presence
in my veins, from heart to fingertips.

So we cross the beck
on unsteady stepping stones
and climb the hill with our feet wet.
There they are ahead of us still,
the wind skimming their laughter.
We do not call,
content to walk together.
In Goathland, without a thousand words,
are spring and love and the brown river
beyond people like us?

ARABIAN GULF, FEBRUARY 1991

It is the darkest death.
I've always been afraid to drown.
Each encounter with the water,
Each swim a test.

Only the cormorant's eye
Lives, freakish bird,
Spilled on the desert edge
From a fractured sky.

On an almond-blossomed hill
Near Jerusalem I learned
To shoot with Mordechai's rifle.
Careless cruelties still

Wound me. The roof of the world
Is black. Hippocampus
Is broken, the imperial
Butterflyfish is humbled.

The coral is sick. The sail-finned
Surgeonfish has no defence.
The gilded violet
Of the damselfish is dimmed.

The dhows are beached. I have always
Found pain in waste. The sheen
Of the silvery pomfret
Is dulled. These are the days

Of torn shelter and more
Than customary lies,
The end of boys and birds,
The spoiling of war.

I remember the balance of steel,
The spit of bullets,
The pale splinters of blossom
That eddied on the hill.

The horizon is lost.
The water burns.
The faces of soldiers are masked
By orders and dust.

These are the days when the yellowtail
And the moonfish have no home.
When the world may drown.
When together right and wrong
May fail the trial by oil.
When I no longer know if life
Or fear or death is natural.

POSTCARD FROM BERLIN

I'm glad you made it to Berlin,
I'm glad you've grown enough.
The train crossed borders never shown on maps,
covering more distance than you think.

I look at Germany through broken glass.
I see you with a gang of ghosts,
flesh and blood and scraps of eerie black
in a naked, ill-lit street.

Bombarded buildings have stood
for fifty years. I understand the past
no better than you, but you have seen less of it.
A daughter's purpose is to look ahead.

You are my messenger. I'll never talk
a fluent way through frontiers
or get beyond the jagged edge.
Die Mauer proclaims, *A chacun son mur*.

My wall encircles images too monstrous
for memory, while you learn to move
through another country. One irony, you write –
the police now guard the synagogue day and night.

NIGHT PASSAGE

The road coils
away from the shore, from the bracelets
of reflection. The mountain's
flank is black
against a less black sky.
The wheels embrace the climb.
Their rolling grip sings in my fingers.
No stars pierce the dark,
and no snow illuminates the pass.

I remember the road home.
The break in the night
is an ice-carved, bouldered glen.
The headlights catch
the tawny run of a river.
Walking in green summer I found
a doe and her fawn
in a shallow bowl of grass
and a buzzard balanced in the wind.

At the next bend is a stone
tumbled from a dyke, and a pair
of roofless gables.
The slope ends at the loch
where a wooden pier rots
softly into the water.
Gentle ruins, temperate,
sure as the yellow aspen and the larch.

The road curves to the crest.
My life keeps pace,
each landmark out of sight.
Anything might be there, an empty house,
a garden thick with foxgloves,
a little grave of a child or a dog,
a boy with bare feet leading a horse,
a woman carrying peats, her basket
high on her back.

Rock looms a fraction
denser than the air. The summit ebbs.
For a moment there is a moon
like a hand open in the night.
Anyone's life. Anyone's road home.

THE YOUNG VISITOR

a green and hummocky field as long as a lifetime
a woman within a black dress
hands in the pockets of a flowered apron
white-haired
her face a delta of red
it is hard to walk on the hummocky green field

the breath of huge cows rolls from their stomachs
they plant their split feet
their tails brush their crusted rumps
the hand leaves the flowered apron to pat a bony shoulder
the gate is heavy
thistles are head high

thin cotton and gumboots
the horse in the yard brings down a hoof massive as a house
a wing of sun shimmers in the byre
decades of grain dance
buckets tilt and clang
the wonder is that the eyes of the beasts remain round and mild
the white head rests on a brown flank
milk plays on metal

the yard is wide as history
the woman carries the bucket to the kitchen
a giant's kettle steams
the oven opens to the soft heat of scones
an army of men's boots tramp
spoons dip into porridge then into milk
they drink tea from saucers
an infinite world is filled

IN MEMORIAM

Dear beast, canny, kenspeckle,
you greet me still. Crazy
they'd say if they knew what I
know of life's relentless spell.

I feel a shadow at the door,
smell the feckless world. Leap
as you used to leap over dyke and gate,
return me to purpose, remind me of grace.

I long for speed on the hill. Mad
they'd say if they shared the spaces in
my head, the caverns, and heard black
and white, bonny peat-pool eyes.

Echoed in the gaffs and gutturals
of this time your guardianship
haunts me. Your ears lift to the sounds
of death. I never answered the questions.

Image of every absence, blur
of bright action, warm to my call.
Each day vividly you pass
trotting at an empty heel.

FIGURE OF A WOMAN

'Figure of a woman, probably a fertility goddess.'
National Museum of Archaeology, Malta

woman fat and fecund
your balloon thighs
might house a family
a clan could cradle
in your belly

your forearms swell
like bladders breasts
blown and windworn
honeyed in the sun
your buttocks are boulders
your shoulders outcrops
and crowning
the matrix mountain
a slender tilted
splinter of a face

limestone lady
of Tarxien mother
made and maker
of men who quarry
in oblivion
your vast cavern

bless if you must
their blind activity
but cherish us
who share your
labyrinthine flesh

lithic madonna
uphold our days
olympian daughter
of contours know
me allow
this poor praise

EYE CONTACT

Eye at the microscope,
blunt hand with blade and forceps,
you slit a finger-sized fish
and examined a thin skein of entrails.
You seemed not to bruise the delicate fin,
the red-edged gill.

I imagined you observing me
through a lens, dissecting sensation,
with a tight frown above the intent eye.
But I spilled like a clear spring
into an underground pool,
beyond sight, beyond the scalpel.

After we parted I saw
almost a stranger on the rim of vision.
You saw an eclipse within your eye,
a darkness that grew. I imagined you
unable to see all that was closest to you,
the kindness, the danger.

After the surgeon, I see
you in dark glasses and dare to touch
your blunt hand. We walk together
and you turn your damaged eye towards me,
and I imagine you see in your head
the way we once loved.

FAMILY

An infant moves starfish limbs
as if under water, as if the familiar
of coral. She is lapped with fond words,
sweetheart, darling, dear.

This is love, her mother knows.
No other passion can compare
with this yearning, the yielding skin
against skin, the tiny finger.

How far beyond this soft kernel
is the love of man. Outside the heart
of things he longs to voyage
in the woman's sea of secrets.

MANAGER

The tangle of no-man's-land
traversed by the manly manager,
manacles in his hand.

I see life. He sees maneaters
and mantraps. He manoeuvres,
his manhood manifest, a world beater.

He is both man-at-arms
and mandarin. I contrive
to stay out of harm's

way. He manhandles manure,
almost mannerly. Mañana, maybe,
we will re-manufacture

mankind. I dream.
The manual of management is tossed
aside. Manners are not what they seem.

I could be mannish, bold,
meet the man of straw
like a man of the world,

clothe myself in manmade camouflage –
but I lack manpower, cannot don
his mantle of subterfuge.

I have no wish to mangle mankind.
This is no manhunt.
Manslaughter is not on my mind.

His mania is manifold. I wait.
He cannot help it.
He is programmed to manipulate.

I take up my pen.
There is more meaning in manuscript
than in man.

TWO GIRLS

Two girls arm in arm in the cold.
They walk slowly under a plume
of warmed air, the breath of their talk.
They bend inwards. I catch their low
serious voices. Shoulders touch.
A pale ellipse of face turns
and two dark holes of eyes meet mine.
Is it men in their depths, mother, father?
The murmur passes down the empty
road. I'm looking back. I was young,
then, afraid to speak, struck
by the tongues of experience, stunned
by what they said would come, the certain
future. Two girls round a corner,
arm in arm, slow, a cloud
of threadbare words attending them.

GEOMETRY
for MB

We talked till late
of circles and straight
lines, of gendered time,
of women living in the round
and the onwardness of men.

And then,
today I made a circle, walked
from Seven Sisters Road
to Upper Street and found
bistros and brasseries
but the shop gone
that cut the butter
into quarter pounds.

The Hare and Hounds
still there, thank God, where
he and I ate lunch
that very first of days.
Then to the Angel
to complete the circle
I'd begun
when I was unforgettably young.

Meanwhile the men
race on, leaving the earth
rather than bend,
as if life were straight,
as if to follow a curve
were to deviate.

RED AFRICA

Water laps red earth
from my baby in the bath.
She has crawled in the dust,
and taken stones in her small hands.

She laughs when black arms
lift her, when she rides a warm
back, down the hill, under the trees.
Snakes drop from the branches, they say.

While the men drink
on the terrace. Today the talk,
tomorrow the revolution. Tracking
the red earth, on the street, in the bars.

My daughter reaches for the red
moth that flies through the window
after the sun has suddenly gone. The men
prise the metal top from another Tusker lager.

A man and woman die
in the dirt. His rimless
glasses slip away from his ebony
eyes. Blood on her smooth and zestful skin.

A vortex of red is stirred
by weaver birds. The roadside
elephants are red. Cars speed to the east,
towards the shifting ocean, trailed by red dust.

ICONOGRAPHY

We drink wine
until the barman's quiet cough
shows us to the door. We share
old times and icons.

The barman takes our glasses
in a single hand and erases
the table. There's a smooth
empty bottle on the bar.

All night we've traded.
A town we knew at different times,
a road we travelled
going different ways.

You with a thrawn wife,
I with the wrong man. A rain
begins. The moon is worn
by the dark, a pale medallion.

What is this barter
of the harvest of years?
Our goodbye is shadowed
by the tall street.

It's too late for equilibrium.
I imagine the buildings
falling and the moon
dust at our feet.

CHURCHYARD, ICKWORTH
for DL

There's a pause in the narrative of lives
to examine graves deep in nettles and chervil.
The air smells of strawberries and the corn
ripens. Friends slowed by the summer,
bonded by the locked doors of the church
at Ickworth and the stones that can be read
and the roads that have brought them there.
Each breath dense with dogrose and honeysuckle.

The place is warmed by death. Bruised
by life and lovers as women mostly
are they've done what has been asked.
The grass here is uncut. It flicks the bare
veined skin, the seeds cling. Only
the two of them wonder at the dead,
the children, the young men in wars. The gate
eases, the catch settles, the sound
of their own voices drifts with the dust.

SUNDOWNER

The sun falls
off the edge of the hot earth
and melts. Colour climbs the sky.
Witnesses lean on the wall

of the bar in Odi, drinking
from cans. The night creeps around
them. The lamp on the counter
is lit. Its luminous island

darkens the corners of the room
and burnishes black skin.
A frayed ribbon of red on the horizon,
the thorn trees gone.

Some yards away the store
lights up and silhouettes throw
faint voices from its open door.
The beer soon becomes warm.
The night is warm.
The talk, spilling over the wall, is warm.

SECRET WATER

A knee on rock,
my cupped hand lifts
water from the burn,
the source of all pleasure,
salted with sweat.

Moments ago I crossed
snow on the fist of Sgurr Mhor
and a skirt of boulders rough
on my fingers. Now water
cool on hot skin
shatters and mingles.

I follow the lustrous
descent of the bright burn,
its leap and rebound,
its witchery when it
seeps into peat and sings
dark under sandstone,

its meeting hugger
mugger the plenty
of springs and the spill
of meltwater, its collision
with the measureless pool.

A knee on rock,
one hand on last year's
brittle heather,
the sun hot and eager,
I drink the brilliant,
cold, secret water.

THE GARDENER

Under the sun he works tender
and methodical, and I watch.
It pleases me as he moves amongst
raspberry canes, purposeful,
at ease, stabbing with the spade,
and pulling weeds. To see him bend
with earthy hands signals affinity.

Actions or words? But there's no choice.
The truth of each can wither,
the brittle flower crushed.
Now he gathers herbs, a gift
from a garden crowded with growth
he has cared for. He stirs
a leaf of ladybirds. His movement
is a love unspoken. My stillness
is a weight of words.

His kiss tastes of mint
and thistles. His fingers
print his garden on my arm. Words
or actions? The sun warms
a silence rippled with roses.

IN PARTICULAR

Today the sea yields
to a whispering veil of mist.
The elements are allies,
yet etch a separateness.

It eddies in the water
as I take my morning's walk
to buy the bread and milk.
My particularity falters

at the blue otherness.
The sun is blunt
but magnificent. The firth
sulks on the surface of the earth.

I believe it covets
the ocean's depth although
it carries a castle slow
on the water, worried by tugs.

The mist is consumed by pale
sky. A wind enters and bends
the white yachts. Every sail
is taut. I tuck a loaf

warm in its paper bag
under my arm. On the hill
a girl waits for a bus,
her high heels thrust

out knees thread-thin.
A pram is wheeled, an Escort
changes gear. A bike spins
a whistling paperboy.

Each an enticing
singularity.
What part have I in this,
hungry for all I see?

My passing scarcely images
the air. Sea and wind
conspire with cloud and land
and I disappear.

ARTHUR'S POEM

Going for a paper
this morning the sun teases
the wet grass and blinds
the low-tide windings of the burn.

On the canal
a life boat *Edith of Yorkshire*,
bound for some relief
or other, breaks

the water's sparkling
picture. The crew
lie on the deck
with eyes half closed.

Two men on the bank
feed a brushwood fire,
and their dog frets
a bone from the butcher's.

In the town a faint
reek of peat. Hands
in the pockets this bright morning,
going for a paper.

SPRING

The trees unclench a little. George
mends my garage door. He weighs
a hammer on his palm. Soon the green
will light each empty-handed branch.

I do not watch him work. Instead
I measure words at my window. Ada
in her slippers hangs out cushion covers.
She culls daffodils. I balance ciphers.

Love and grief, courage, joy.
Life is sensational. An orange-breasted
bird commands the fence. George
brings silence with his can of oil.

Emblems assert a spaceless presence.
From her garden Ada waves.
For spring I choose a flyting finch.
George knocks. The job is done, he says.

ACTS OF LOVE

Of all love's acts how odd
is this supremacy. Oh
it shakes me sometimes,
drives me beyond borders,

but more elusive union
also capsizes caution,
the free fall of a whisper,
a freighted space
between two hands, too frail
to celebrate it seems.

Now something new.
African voices on a hillside,
the tenderest song I've ever heard,
as a coffin is lowered,
a grave filled, and trees
tentatively green,
reach improbably
out of the parched earth.